T0169374

Soul of Barcelona

A GUIDE TO 30 EXCEPTIONAL EXPERIENCES

WRITTEN BY FANY PÉCHIODAT AND VINCENT MOUSTACHE
ILLUSTRATED BY VINCENT MOUSTACHE
PHOTOS BY JUAN JEREZ

JONGLEZ PUBLISHING

travel guides

'A THOUSAND PERFUMES
AND A THOUSAND
COLOURS – BARCELONA
IS A CITY OF
A THOUSAND FACES'

JOAN MANUEL SERRAT
"BARCELONA I JO"

WHAT YOU WON'T FIND
IN THIS GUIDE

- a map of the Barcelona Metro
- the direct number for Casa Milà
- the most touristy place for tapas
- a list of medications to bring

WHAT YOU WILL FIND
IN THIS GUIDE

- a breakfast of hot chocolate and charcuterie
  (where Albert Adrià goes in the morning)
- a hotel in a bakery
- a secret jazz concert in buildings designed by Gaudí
- the city's best churros
- the art of eating *calçots*, available only between January
  and March

Why do we love Barcelona?

- Because it's a city that feels like it's always on holiday: sun, beaches, outdoor drinks all year round.
- Because you'll find Banksy side-by-side with Gaudí; in this city, there's poetry everywhere.
- Because the Adrià brothers have shaped an entire generation of young chefs, the heirs to elBulli, who are opening up scores of restaurants, reinventing the local cuisine with humour, winks, an anti-conformist attitude, and revamped tapas...
- Because there are rooftops everywhere, and stairs and elevators on every street corner to take you there for a drink and to admire the city from above.
- Because the whole city is a party: from intimate neighbourhood gatherings (with human pyramids) to popular parties and clubs, Barcelona is the city of 'Fiesta Mayor'.

We tasted everything, searched high and low, and explored all over ... Here are our 30 favourite experiences to unlock Barcelona's secret doors, capture its heartbeat, and uncover its soul.

SYMBOLS USED IN
'SOUL OF BARCELONA'

< 20 euros

20 to 60 euros

> 60 euros

you'll need a car
to get there

reservation
recommended

take advantage
of the terrace

staff, a bit rough around the edges,
but that's part of the appeal

30 EXPERIENCES

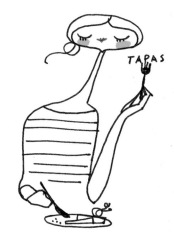

A TINY ESTABLISHMENT
FOR TAPAS

Tiny, noisy, frenetic … this pocket-sized bodega is an institution renowned throughout Spain.

You won't find any tables here – it's standing room only. Let yourself be tempted by a glass of the house vermouth as the tapas appear and disappear at full throttle. Red bell peppers, foie gras, camembert with honey, grilled artichoke, cod, sweet and savoury pintxo … Quim's tapas are inspired creations – he nails it every time, and his daring recipes soon pop up all across the country. Some Barcelonians even call Quimet y Quimet the 'elBulli of tapas'.

Definitely don't skip the salmon with yogurt and honey truffles paired (de rigueur) with a glass of pink cava, a fresh and bubbly rosé that will banish all thoughts of prosecco from your mind.

 QUIMET & QUIMET
CARRER DEL POETA CABANYES, 25
08004 BARCELONA

MON–FRI: noon / 4pm – 6pm / 10:30pm
SAT–SUN: Closed

PHOTO CREDIT: VINCENT MOUSTACHE

THE MICRO-CITY
CASA BONAY

'Casa Bonay is more than just a hotel; it's a micro city' – as this opening line from an article in *The Telegraph* suggests, Casa Bonay is far more than a hotel: it's a coffee shop, bookshop (Barcelona's smallest), cocktail bar, several restaurants, rooftop bar... and, above all, a platform for all the local talent, since everything here is 100 % Made in Barcelona.

Ines Miró-Sans, the hotel's founder, trained at the Ace Hotel in New York so she knows better than anyone that a hotel is first and foremost a living space with a programme. Even if you aren't staying at the hotel, check out the events on its site: guest DJs at the weekend, documentary screenings, concerts, parties, curry nights, book presentations – you're bound to find what you're looking for to take a break at Casa Bonay.

CASA BONAY
GRAN VIA DE LES CORTS CATALANES, 700
08010 BARCELONA

+34 935 458 070
casabonay.com

PHOTO CREDITS: BEN HOLBROOK

THE ART OF EATING
CALÇOTS

Each country has its culinary curiosities, and eating *calçots* will throw even periwinkle-eaters for a loop!

Calçot season – exclusively between January and March – is an unmissable gastronomic event for Barcelonians.

Calçots – elongated, sweet onions that look a bit like little leeks – are eaten grilled with Romesco sauce, a mixture of almonds, hazelnuts, tomatoes, and garlic. To die for.

It's when you get around to actually eating these famous *calçots* that things get interesting. There's a whole ritual involving donning a bib and setting aside any pretence of elegance and glamour.

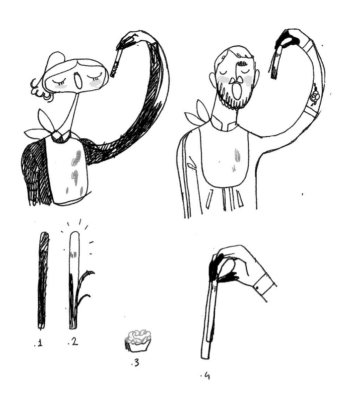

SO HOW DOES IT ACTUALLY WORK?

Step 1 : Peel the skin off the grilled *calçots*. Obviously your hands are completely black now ... Barbecue style. Awesome.

Step 2: Dip the *calçot* in delicious Romesco sauce. This is the coolest part of the exercise.

Step 3: Dangle the full length of *calçot* over your head, open your mouth and aim for your piehole while trying to avoid making a total mess!

Step 4: Savour this delicate and finger-licking tidbit ... of slightly barbaric appeal.

You get the message: We love *calçots*. They're gourmet, addictive, fun to eat in company, and available only a few months a year – so, if you get a chance to try them, don't let it pass you by.

> EL MIRADOR DE CAN CASES
FOR FIRST-RATE *CALÇOTS*

Calçots are truly an insider's treat. Not many travelers even know they exist – not least because you can't get them everywhere. That's why we love this place on a hilltop just a few minutes drive from the city centre.

Not many tourists know about Mirador de Can Cases, so you'll find mostly locals, here to indulge in *calçots* and other grilled delicacies. Keep in mind that this type of onion is only available from January to March.

Miss this window and your belly might well be miffed – and you won't have anyone to blame for it but yourself.

 EL MIRADOR DE CAN CASES
CAMÍ DE CAN CASES, 15
08196 LES PLANES - BARCELONA

WED–THU: 11am / 5pm
FRI: 11am / 11:30pm
SAT: noon / 11:30pm

SUN: noon / 6pm
MON–TUE: Closed

JAZZ TO THE RHYTHM
OF GAUDÍ

The name Gaudí will never sound the same to you again after you've attended this magical jazz festival, which is held once a year in buildings designed by the nec plus ultra of Catalonian architects. A glass of champagne in your hand, jazz notes reverberating off modernist edifices beneath the stars ... What more could you ask for?

CASA BATLLÓ
LAS NOCHES MAGICAS
PASSEIG DE GRÀCIA, 43
08007 BARCELONA

+34 932 160 306   casabatllo.es/ca/venda-entrades/visita-nits-magiques
info@casabatllo.cat

PEIX

Pan Tostado	1·80	Cal Romana	950
Bomba	2·00	Arengue	350
Morcillas	3·90	Sardinas	550
Xameinyóns	—	Barat	600
Bacon	2·00	Calamar	650-9
Habas	2·40	Pulpo	600
Butifarra	3·60	Recortes Pulpo	4·200
Chorizo	3·60	Bacalao	650
Cap i Pota	4·70	Escabeche	550
Amanida	4·0	Esqueixada	46
Judías	2·00	Samoés	
Garbanzos	3·40	Escaitarlos	11·40
Ensaladilla		Bunyols Bac	5·00
	1·56	Tellerines	
	3·	Navalles	

THE GRANNY ADORED
BY TOP CHEFS

This small family restaurant harbours a treasure that goes by the name of Palmira. In the guise of a rustic, irresistible little granny, she's actually one of the country's most respected chefs – that's how authentic she's managed to keep her cooking. Since she founded her establishment in 1944, all the top chefs have made pilgrimages there to (re)discover the taste of real traditional tapas, like their own grandmothers undoubtedly made.

Surrounded by her family, Palmira offers a short, no-frills menu that always features local and seasonal products – including bomba, breaded potato croquettes that'll knock your socks off. If they're in season, the artichokes will make your heart melt. The *alubias con sepia* (cuttlefish and beans) and *recortes de pulpo* (squid) are also well worth the trip.

 LA COVA FUMADA
CARRER DEL BALUARD, 56
08003 BARCELONA

MON-TUE: 9am / 3pm
THU-FRI: 9am / 3pm – 6pm / 8pm

SAT: 9am / 1pm
WED-SUN: Closed

PALO MARKET FEST,
A MARKET UNLIKE ANY OTHER

Nothing would make you suspect that a market featuring Barcelona's most influential small creators is held once a month here, at the heart of this industrial neighbourhood.

From vendors of costume jewelry and more or less experimental fashion to up-and-coming DJs and obscure food – the melting-pot of creatives here today will give you a taste of the cultural and party scene of tomorrow.

These artists and artisans congregate here to see and be seen, so remember their names because you might stumble across the Cristóbal Balenciaga of the 21st century.

 PALO MARKET FEST FLEA MARKET
CARRER DELS PELLAIRES, 30 - 38
08019 BARCELONA

The first week-end of the month
SAT-SUN: 11am / 9pm

palomarketfest.com

PHOTO CREDIT: FANY PÉCHIODAT

THE TAPAS
SANCTUARY

Try to arrive early at Cañete so you can nab a spot at the narrow and neverending bar. It's the perfect spot for leisurely watching the cooks with their superb toques, who seem straight out of the animated film *Ratatouille*, and brisk waiters dressed in white whose enthusiasm is contagious. Guaranteed entertainment.

On the menu: *pan con tomate*, aubergine chips, *jamón de Bellota*, *gambas a la plancha*, artichoke omelette dusted with truffle ... Typically Barcelonian tapas, simple and potent recipes that put the emphasis on flavour and conviviality.

CAÑETE
CARRER DE LA UNIÓ, 17
08001 BARCELONA

MON–SAT: 1pm / midnight | +34 932 703 458
SUN: Closed | barcanete.com

A PIZZERIA
IN A CAR PARK

It may feel like you're entering a garage, but you'll definitely know you're in a pizzeria once you're inside: Welcome to Parking Pizza.

During the day, the loft-style industrial beauty of this space will surprise you with its calm and relaxing vibe. At night, you'll almost think you're in one of Berlin's underground clubs. The wood-oven cooked pizzas are delicious, especially the one with burrata and stracciatella.

And for a taste of the easternmost Mediterranean cuisine you can pop right next door to the pizzeria's 'little brother', Parking Pita.

 PARKING PIZZA
PASSEIG DE SANT JOAN, 56
08009 BARCELONA

SUN-THU: 1pm / 4pm – 8pm / 11pm
FRI-SAT: 1pm / 4pm – 8pm / midnight

parkingpizza.com

09

SPEND A NIGHT
IN A BAKERY

8 am. The light filters into your room. You open your eyes. You're barely conscious when the scent of croissants fresh from the oven lures you out of bed.

The alarm clock has just gone off at the Praktik Hotel in Barcelona. A hotel-cum-bakery that smells deliciously of oven-hot bread. The lobby? Right between the baguettes, pies, and cakes ... The elevator? At the back to the right, behind the chouquettes. The reception? At the end of the bread counter of the famous Baluard Barceloneta, the city's best bakery.

Less than 10€ will buy you a complete breakfast with all the bread and pastries you can eat. Good morning, Barcelona!

PRAKTIK BAKERY
CARRER DE PROVENÇA, 279
08037 BARCELONA

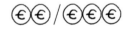

+34 934 880 061
hotelpraktikbakery.com

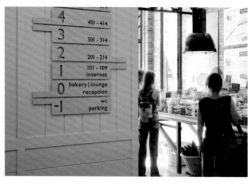

THE BEST
PATATAS BRAVAS
IN BARCELONA

> **EL TOMÁS**

WHERE BARCELONIANS HAVE BEEN GOING FOR 40 YEARS

Located in the Sarrià neighbourhood, El Tomás is the kind of place that plays its cards close to its chest. Far from the trendy rooftops and bars, El Tomás de Sarrià is simply the place where, for 40 years now, all of Barcelona has been going for the city's best *patatas bravas*.

Hand peeled and cut, El Tomás's *patatas* are tender to perfection and served with a generous coating of aïoli or delicious chili sauce.

A little warning for nightbirds: El Tomás doesn't live on Spanish time and closes at 10 pm! So remember to come early so you don't end up having to go home hungry.

 EL TOMÁS DE SARRIÀ
CARRER MAJOR DE SARRIÀ, 49
08017 BARCELONA

MON–SAT: 12:30 pm / 4pm – 6:30 pm / 10pm
SUN: Closed

> LA MUNDANA
CONTEMPORARY *PATATAS BRAVAS*

Leave the Kinder eggs to the kids – presenting Tapas Surprise!

The menu at this confounding restaurant features dishes that are as traditional and integral to the Catalan identity as they come. But, while you may have ordered patatas bravas, it will take you a moment to recognise them when they appear in the form of an ultra-graphic chocolate or caramel eclair. Same thing for the paella, which shows up half-a-centimetre thick on a square surface but is still creamy and tasty.

Incredibly playful, this trompe-l'oeil cuisine is the fruit of the imagination of Alain Guiard and Marc Martín, who cut their teeth in Europe's most prestigious kitchens and have won numerous prizes for their catering service. Respected by all of Barcelona's great chefs, they've brought their talents and sense of humour together at La Mundana, where everything is faux traditional but genuinely exquisite.

LA MUNDANA
CARRER DEL VALLESPIR, 93
08014 BARCELONA

MON–SUN: 1pm / 3:30 pm – 8pm / 11:30 pm

+34 934 088 023
lamundana.cat

PHOTO CREDIT: FANY PÉCHIODAT

HAVE A BATH
BENEATH THE CITY

While you're in Barcelona you might be tempted to indulge in some R&R. Luckily you can escape the noise of the city while staying right in the heart of it at this underground spa located in an 18th-century warehouse in the El Born neighbourhood.

In this sanctum dedicated to the pleasures of relaxation, several pools of various temperatures allow you to relax both body and mind, before or after a well-earned massage. What's more, this temple of wellbeing is open until 2am on Friday and Saturday and until midnight during the rest of the week. A getaway you should always keep in mind for after a long night of tapas.

 AIRE DE BARCELONA
PASSEIG DE PICASSO, 22
08003 BARCELONA

SUN–THU: 9am / 11:30pm
FRI–SAT: 9am / 2am

+34 932 955 743
beaire.com

THE MICHELIN-STARRED RESTAURANT
THAT'S ALL ABOUT FUN

Inhalable whisky pie, edible cotton you can pick directly from the stalk, translucent pasta – this restaurant is all about having fun. This gourmet eatery rich in flavours and intensity is the brainchild of three former chefs from the acclaimed elBulli: Mateu Casaña, Oriol Castro, and Eduard Xatruch.

To ensure maximum enjoyment of their 30-dish cycle of gastronomic poems, the cooks won't let you look at the menu or google it in advance.

A disfrutar (= enjoy)!

DISFRUTAR
CARRER DE VILLARROEL, 163
08009 BARCELONA

SUN–THU: 9am / 4pm – 8pm / 11pm
FRI–SAT: 9am / 4pm – 8pm / midnight

disfrutarbarcelona.com
Tasting menu – 180 euros (without wine)

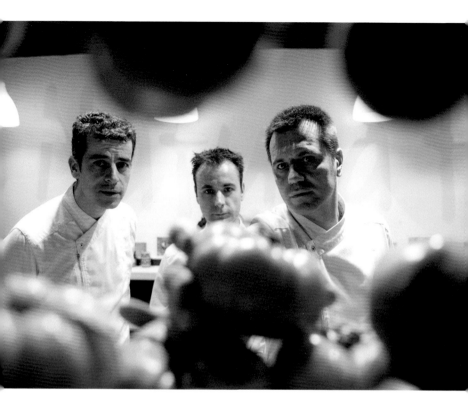

THE COOLEST CLUB
IN THE WORLD

Soho House is a members' club that's opening incredible spaces, reserved for creative and artistic talents, all over the world. Here, you can work, eat, sleep, and party with members, whose creativity seems to know no bounds.

Soho House has two locations in Barcelona:

- A hotel located in an 18th-century antique-pink building at the heart of the city's Barri Gotic (Gothic Quarter). Good news: the hotel and Cecconi restaurant are open to non-members (by reservation), so you can try their classic pasta alle vongole (with clams) and schmooze.

 SOHO HOUSE
PLAÇA DEL DUC DE MEDINACELI, 4
08002 BARCELONA

+34 932 204 600
sohohousebarcelona.com

- The Little Beach House, located 30 minutes by car, near Garraf. Your mission: track down a member who'll invite you to eat paella as you dangle your feet in the water. Definitely worth a trip!

 LITTLE BEACH HOUSE BARCELONA
CARRER MIRADOR DEL PORT, 1
08871 GARRAF - BARCELONA

+34 935 221 552
sohohousebarcelona.com

REDFISH
MOLL DE LA MARINA, S/N
08005 BARCELONA

WED-THU & SUN: 11am / 8pm
FRI-SAM: noon / 11pm
SUN: 11am / 8pm

+34 931 716 894
redfishbcn.com

Paella frente al mar ⭐

EAT PAELLA
AT THE WATER'S EDGE

No introduction necessary: Paella is an icon of Spanish cuisine. We found a restaurant that's both at the heart of the city and at the water's edge, a small house that's an utter anomaly on this beach. Enjoy the tapas and legendary paella with a glass in hand and the silhouette of Barcelona on the horizon.

A BRIEF GUIDE
TO PAELLA

While the original recipe may be from Valencia, not all of its derivatives
go by the name of paella: some are called *arroz* (rice)
and others *fideuá* (because they're made with vermicelli).

To help you out, here's a brief guide to paella:

PAELLA: According to the traditional
recipe, only vegetables (including artichokes,
bell peppers, and tomatoes), green beans,
garrofó (a type of large white bean),
chicken, and rabbit go into this dish,
which is originally from Valencia.

MEAT PAELLA: Generally contains
primarily chicken, though you'll
definitely also find other kinds
of meat. This spicier version of the
dish comes mainly from Spain's
inland regions:
a real country dish.

SEAFOOD PAELLA: Composed of squid, clams,
mussels, prawns, and other seafood,
it's sometimes even served with fish.
Obviously, this version comes chiefly
from the country's coastal regions.

MIXED PAELLA: Combines meat and seafood,
especially squid and prawns.
This land-and-sea dish is also often
found in France.

ARROZ NEGRO: This dish derives
its characteristic colour from
squid ink. A mix of squid, prawns,
and garlic, it's usually served with aïoli.

ARROZ AL HORNO: Unlike paella
(which roughly means 'cooked in a pan'),
this dish is cooked in the oven,
with plenty of meat, sausage,
and chickpeas.

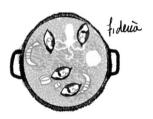

FIDEUÁ: This may look like paella from
a distance, but the squid, prawns, and mussels
in this dish come with noodles and fish soup
instead of rice. It's sometimes served
with aïoli and never contains meat.

ENJOY A COCKTAIL
IN A RETRO BAR

Welcome to early 20th-century Barcelona, the perfect era for enjoying a cocktail made with flowers or peanuts. More than just a cocktail bar that uses exceptional ingredients, La Confitería 1912 is virtually a museum of Art nouveau-inspired decor.

You'll find another alternative for exploring Barcelona's raffish side a few blocks away at Bar Marsella.

LA CONFITERÍA 1912
CARRER DE SANT PAU, 128
08001 BARCELONA

MON–THU: 7pm / 3am
FRI–SAT: 6pm / 3:30 am
SUN: 5pm / 3am

BAR MARSELLA
CARRER DE SANT PAU, 65
08001 BARCELONA

MON–SUN: 6pm / 2am

BARCELONA'S
TREASURE TROVE

Just a stone's throw away from Barcelona lies the small town of Sant Cugat and its flea market. Here you'll find antiques dealers, artisans, and designers who will make you want to redecorate your entire apartment with the bargains you dig up here.

After wandering amidst a thousand and one decorative treasures you can sit down at one of the many tapas bars or food trucks – which are also inspiring and inspired in their design.

 MERCANTIC
AV. DE RIUS I TAULET, 120
08173 SANT CUGAT DEL VALLÈS – BARCELONA

TUE–SAT: 10am / 8pm
SUN: 10am / 4pm
MON: Closed

mercantic.com

IT'S VERMOUTH O'CLOCK

Vermouth in Barcelona is like G&T in the UK: a classic pre-dinner drink, not to say an institution. So Barcelona's *vermuterías* are the equivalent of London's small pubs – but with a generous splash of Spanish sun!

Barcelona's best neighbourhood bar, Calders, has one of the loveliest terraces for enjoying a drink, served with olives, as is customary. You can sip it with a side of squid or other tinned tidbits.

If you head here after dark, we recommend arriving early so you can snag a nice table outdoors and order a special Vermouth menu – ensuring you'll make the most of the local happy hour.

CALDERS
CARRER DEL PARLAMENT, 25
08015 BARCELONA

MON–THU: 5pm / 1am
FRI–SUN: 11am / 2am
SUN: 11am / midnight

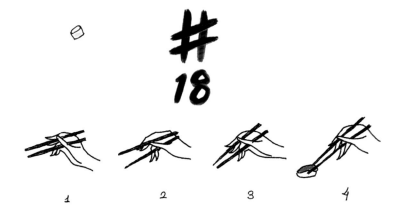

LA BOQUERÍA MARKET'S
POCKET-SIZED RESTAURANT

Arnau Muñío, an erstwhile chef at the great elBulli, decided to open this restaurant of his dreams beneath the arcades of this Barcelonian market. He wanted to serve *cocina de mercat*: the sort of market cuisine his grandmother would cook using whatever she'd found at the stalls that day.

There are only eight seats around the small wooden counter to ensure that the unique menu gets its full due. Since sharing this sort of culinary adventure can only bring people closer together, there's a good chance you'll end up best friends with your neighbours at the table.

DIREKTE BOQUERÍA
CARRER DE LES CABRES, 13
08001 BARCELONA

€€€

TUE–THU: 1:15pm / 3:15pm – 7pm / 2:30am
FRI–SAT: 1:15pm / 3:15pm – 8pm / 10pm
SUN–MON: Closed

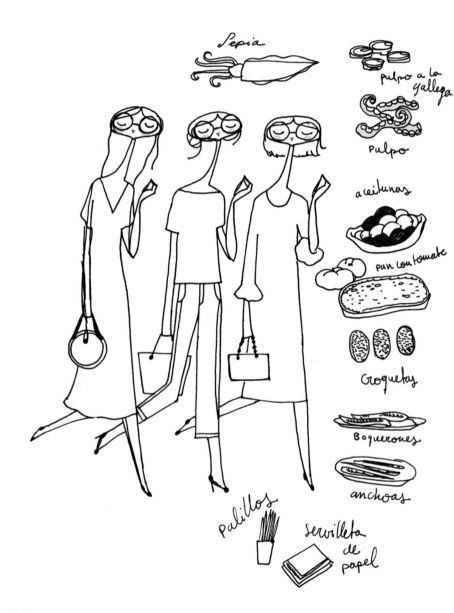

Sepia

pulpo a la gallega

pulpo

aceitunas

pan con tomate

croquetas

Boquerones

anchoas

palillos

servilleta de papel

The temple of Barcelona, La Boquería is teeming with artisans selling fruits and vegetables, charcuterie, seafood, wine, and good preserved foods. You'll also find a tapas bar, street food that's beyond tempting, and food shops. Here are our top picks:

- Torrons Vicens. **405.**
  For stocking up on *turrón* (Spanish white nougat).
- Olives i conserves El Pinyol. **230.**
  For olives and quality preserved foods.
- Cansaladeria Can Vila. **162.**
  The *jamón* paradise.
- Embotits Montse. **173.**
  The nec plus ultra of Spanish delicatessens.
- Pinotxo. **465.**
  A delicious tapas bar, very popular with Barcelonians.
- La Carte del Vins. **450.**
  A wine shop that always offers great advice.
- Ous de Calaf. **323.**
  To help you decide between the chicken and the egg.
- Fruites i Verdures Vidal Pons. **512.**
  A greengrocer bursting with colours.
- Peixateria Manolo. **759.**
  A fishmonger specialised in oysters.
- Fantasía de Pimientos. **610 - 611 - 612.**
  The paradise of peppers, from sweet to spicy.

La Boquería has created this interactive map to help you find your way around, with more information about each stall: **www.boqueria.barcelona/paradas-mercado**

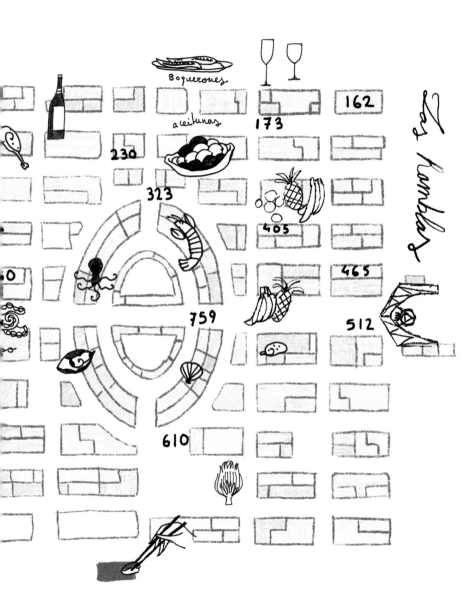

Boquerones

aceitunas

230

162

173

323

405

465

512

759

610

Las Ramblas

IF YOU'RE A SUCKER
FOR STATIONERY ...

Picture an ocean of notebooks, papers, pens, and pencils: Raima is, simply put, the biggest stationery shop in Europe. It was founded in 1986 by Núria Raja in this very building, which dates to 1913 – with many pieces of vintage and upcycled furniture that are still there to this day.

Don't forget to go up to the 4th floor, where you'll find a little-known terrace with a breathtaking view over the rooftops of this historic city.

RAIMA
CARRER COMTAL, 27
08002 BARCELONA

MON–FRI: 9:45am / 9pm
SAT: 10am / 9pm
SUN: Closed

raimapapers.cat

Gino

Cava Tinto · Blanco · Rosado

WHERE TO GRAB
A DRINK

This wine bar-cum-dining cellar is embedded in the reactor core, on the thoroughfare that separates El Born and La Ribera. As soon as you enter, a long display table of wines gets straight to the heart of the matter. Next up is a second bar, followed by two rooms that share a third bar, which also serves as a 'serving hatch' for the open kitchen, where the chef keeps a watchful eye on every plate.

In short, you get the picture: This is the kind of chaotic place we love, rough around the edges but serving Barcelona's best natural wines. Bar Brutal also has the city's best *burrata* and other tapas that are as nummy as they are no-nonsense.

BAR BRUTAL
CARRER DE LA BARRA DE FERRO, 1
08005 BARCELONA

MON–SUN: 10am / 7pm

+34 932 954 797
cancisa.cat

EAT BETTER,
LIVE LONGER

In a country where charcuterie is the star of almost every plate, the vegetarian restaurant Flax & Kale has nevertheless managed to gain cult status in Barcelona.

The woman behind it, Teresa Carles, has your best interests at heart. She opened her first restaurant in 1979 with a simple guiding principle: to serve Catalan family cooking with local ingredients, healthy recipes, and a vegetarian menu. Her credo: Eat better, be happier, live longer.

There's something for everyone here: gluten free, crudivore, vegan ... Remember to reserve a spot on the terrace to make the most of the sun and scents from the vegetable garden!

 FLAX & KALE - TALLERS
CARRER DELS TALLERS, 74B
08001 BARCELONA

MON–FRI: 9am / 11:30pm   flaxandkale.com
SAT–SUN: 9:30am / 11:30pm

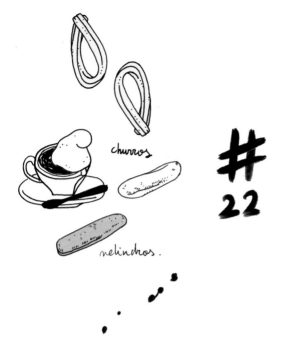

churros

#
22

nelindros.

HOT CHOCOLATE
AND CHARCUTERIE

Don't let the modest façade and dated look fool you: Granja Viader is one of *the* main spots of Barcelona's culinary scene.

Founded in 1870, this erstwhile dairy is now an institution where Barcelonians cross paths with travelers who've come here to discover Granja's mythic hot chocolate, a thick and dense beverage topped with a generous dollop of whipped cream ....

GRANJA VIADER
CARRER D'EN XUCLÀ, 4
08001 BARCELONA

MON–SUN: 9am / 1:15 pm – 5pm / 9:15pm
Closed on Sunday and holidays

+34 933 183 486

You can pair this decadent indulgence with another sweet treat, from churros to *melindros* (ladyfingers), but definitely don't miss trying a slice of ham or piece of cheese with quince jam and a touch of fleur de sel. Absolute heaven.

Don't be surprised if you run into the Michelin-starred chef Albert Adrià since he's the one who told us about this somewhat secret spot, where he loves to have breakfast. For the record, Picasso himself came to Granja for hot chocolate ... The place where great connaisseurs converge.

AN ABUNDANCE
OF GREENERY

A veritable oasis of greenery and refreshments in the middle of the industrial district of Poblenou, Espai Joliu is worth a visit. Already at the entrance, plants placed on palettes set the tone – which is soon confirmed by the contrast between the concrete walls, reclaimed furniture, and wholesome pastries.

Here you'll find specialty coffees, a wide variety of teas, fresh juices, and delicious little dishes, including numerous vegetarian and vegan options. All in a decor that's so incredibly Instagrammable it'll make your fingers itch for your phone.

 ESPAI JOLIU
CARRER DE BADAJOZ, 95
08005 BARCELONA

MON: 3pm / 7pm
TUE–FRI: 9:30am / 7pm
SAT: 10am / 3pm

PHOTO CREDIT: BEN HOLBROOK

HURTLE DOWN THE HILLS
ON A BIKE

In a city as sunny as this, it would be a shame not to spend as much time as possible outdoors. Not just so you can get your fill of Vitamin D and sea air but also to get to know the city's neighbourhoods and contours better than you can by car.

The following is a list of places and streets that are especially fun to discover on foot, by bike, or even on a skateboard:

. Passeig de Sant Joan, Passeig de Lluís Companys
  and Parc de la Ciutadella
. Rambla de Poblenou and Passeig Marítim in the Barceloneta district
. Plaça dels Àngels, across from the Barcelona Museum of
  Contemporary Art (MACBA)
. Rambla Catalunya and Enrique Granados
. Diagonal Avenue
. The streets and parks of the Gràcia district
. Passeig de Colom, The Maritime Museum and Barceloneta
. Plaça d'Espanya
. Montjuïc hill and castle (Montjuïc Cable Car even offers a unique
  bird's-eye panoramic view of Barcelona)
. Passeig de Gràcia

To rent a bike: **www.rentabikebcn.com/index.html**

You can also rent an electric bike at **ebikesexperience.com** and ride in Collserola Natural Park to overlook Barcelona and have lunch in the secret *masías*.

PHOTO CREDIT: BEN HOLBROOK

25

DISCOVER
THE WONDERFUL WORLD
OF ALBERT ADRIÀ

There's a before and after Albert Adrià in Barcelona. Since closing elBulli, the best restaurant in the world, which he helmed with his brother in the 2000s, he has adapted all of their creative methods for various new restaurants. Some are Catalanian themed, others Japanese or Mexican, but each of them takes the same incredible care to surprise and guarantee each customer an 'aha moment'. Albert makes the rounds of his seven restaurants to taste the dishes on the various menus. He has kept his inner child alive, dreaming about his restaurants before creating them. 'When I cook, I'm the happiest guy in the world', he explains. He has managed to surround himself with a team in his own image, including in particular the explosive Xavi Alba, the dining room manager of Tickets.

A CULINARY FUNFAIR

The most iconic of these restaurants is the first, Tickets, where you can eat the most creative tapas in the world in a circus-like ambiance: upside-down sandwiches, trompe-l'œil peanuts, spherical olives – all in an atmosphere that's reminiscent of a funfair.

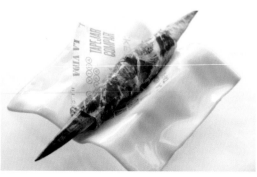

TICKETS
AV. DEL PARAL·LEL, 164
08015 BARCELONA

€€€

TUE-FRI: 7pm / 10:30pm
SAT: 1pm / 3pm - 7pm / 10:30pm
SUN-MON: Closed

elbarri.com/restaurant/tickets

After Tickets, Albert opened an old-fashioned *vermutería*, Bodega 1900, where he offers the typically Barcelonian experience of vermouth and tapas. This was followed by Pakta, where he presents his interpretation of nikkei cuisine (a fusion of Peruvian and Japanese cooking), including incredible ceviche. Then came Hoja Santa, where you can also try revamped tacos with Adrià sauce and tequila-based cocktails. Finally, there's Enigma, a gastronomic experience so outlandish it's impossible to describe: a ballet of 40 dishes eaten over the course of four hours and accompanied by spectacular changes in scenery.

BODEGA 1900
CARRER DE TAMARIT, 91
08015 BARCELONA
TUE-SAT: 1pm / 4pm - 7pm / 10:30pm
SUN-MON: Closed

ENIGMA
SEPÚLVEDA, 38-40
08015 BARCELONA
TUE-FRI: 7pm / 9:30pm
SAT: 1pm / 2:30pm - 7pm / 9:30pm
SUN-MON: Closed

PAKTA
CARRER LLEIDA, 5
08015 BARCELONA
TUE-FRI: 7pm / 10:30pm
SAT: 1:30pm / 3pm - 8pm / 10pm
SUN-MON: Closed

HOJA SANTA
AVDA. DE MISTRAL, 54
08015 BARCELONA
TUE-FRI: 7pm / 10pm
SAT: 1pm / 2:30pm - 7pm / 10:30pm
SUN-MON: Closed

- ALBERT ADRIÀ -

"I am what I cook and I cook what I am", Albert Adrià talks to us about the influence of Barcelona and his connection to the city.

You could have settled in any city in the world – so why did you choose Barcelona?

I love living in Barcelona, it's truly my city. Life here is very Mediterranean; it's sitting on a terrace drinking vermouth and eating tapas – everything I love. My favourite street is Calle Parlament because of its very Barcelonian look and because a good meal or glass of wine is never far away. When I head home at the end of an evening shift, I go out of my way to take this street because it inspires my imagination.

What are your favourite experiences in Barcelona?

Simple and authentic spots like the tapas bar Xampanyet (even if it's always packed) and the restaurant La Cova Fumada (see page 31).

What's your favourite breakfast place?

La Granja Viader (see page 92) in the Gothic quarter El Raval, right near Las Ramblas. They invented a hot chocolate recipe that's been known as the best throughout Barcelona for five generations. I often go there to start my day.

In what way do your dishes reflect the culture of Barcelona?

Of all my dishes, I think the spherical olives most resemble the city of Barcelona: explosive, surprising, memorable. If I had to put this city on a plate, it would be a big spoon with a spherical olive on it.

BARCELONA'S
CONCEPT STORE

Argentinian designer Jaime Beriestain considers his concept store an extension of his home: 'Mi casa es su casa'.

People come here to lounge around, have some tea, buy pretty crockery, a book, or a bouquet of flowers, pick up gifts for friends, and even to try dishes from a menu Beriestain himself co-created with his chef.

JAIME BERIESTAIN CONCEPT STORE
PAU CLARIS, 167
08037 BARCELONA

MON–FRI: 10am / 9pm
SAT: 11am / 9pm
SUN: 11:30 am / 7:30 pm

- JAMIE BERIESTAIN -

Jaime Beriestain arrived in Barcelona in 2000 and founded his own interior architecture studio two years later. Beriestain established his own café-cum-concept store right near one of the city's landmarks, Gaudí's La Pedrera. We met him there to talk about his design work (which includes both decorative objects and furniture – and even recipes) and why this city inspires him so much.

You could have settled in any city in the world – so why did you choose Barcelona?

Barcelona is an enormous inspiration to me. Both because it's one of the most interesting cities in Spain and because it's so Mediterranean. And obviously also because it's so full of opportunities.

In what way does your design style reflect the soul of Barcelona?

Because we see the city in all its modernity and cosmo-politanism. In a reflection of Barcelona, which is always moving forward, we're constantly proposing new designs based on thousands of possible materials.

We also respect the urban planning and long history of the houses and buildings that make this city what it is today.

If you had to choose
a place or experience
that defines Barcelona, what
would it be?
For me. Barcelona means so many different things. But the aspect of the city I love to recommend most is its interest in culture and contemporary art.

We have brilliant museums like the MACBA and Joan Miró Foundation. But also galleries like Miquel Alzueta and Galeria Senda – and so many more!

What's your
favourite breakfast
place?
My own café! We serve breakfast that's both gourmet and healthy. What more can you ask for?

TO THE END
OF THE NIGHT

1. DANCE TILL DAWN

Partying is fundamental to Barcelona. This city stays up long after the sun goes down, with the nightlife carrying on in bars and clubs it's hard to choose between. Here's our selection of places for carousing to the end of the night.

SALA APOLO
CARRER NOU DE LA RAMBLA, 113
08004 BARCELONA
2 rooms, 2 vibes
MON–SUN: 7pm / 5 h 30
Check the website
sala-apolo.com

JAMBOREE
PLAÇA REIAL, 17
08002 BARCELONA
Jazz club
MON–SUN: 7:30pm / midnight

SIDECAR
PLAÇA REIAL, 7
08002 BARCELONA
300-person club
WED: 7pm / 2:30am
THU: 7pm / 5am
FRI–SAT: 7pm / 6am
SUN & TUE: Closed

MOOG
CARRER DE L'ARC DEL TEATRE, 3
08002 BARCELONA
Electro club
SUN–THU: midnight / 5am
FRI–SAT: midnight / 6am

RAZZMATAZZ
CARRER DELS ALMOGÀVERS, 122
08018 BARCELONA
Barcelona's biggest nightclub, with 5 rooms
THU–FRI: 12:30am / 5am
SAT–SUN: 1am / 6am
MON & WED: Closed

Fiesta

2. A CHURROS AFTERPARTY

> Churrería J. Argilés

This food truck right by the exit of the Marina subway station hasn't moved an inch in almost 60 years. Surrounded by streets and trams, Churrería J. Argilés's location itself is already an experience. Open 24 hours at the weekend, it's the perfect place to refuel after having danced the night away, especially since its churros are amongst the best in the city. Something the locals clearly know!

 CHURRERÍA J. ARGILÉS
CARRER DE LA MARINA, 107
08018 BARCELONA

TUE–FRI: 8:15am / 9:30pm
SAT: Open 24 hours
SUN: Midnight / 9:30pm
MON: Closed

> Churrería San Román

A Barcelona institution, this churrería is run by Manuel San Román, a family man who's been perfecting his personal recipe since he was 12-years old. In other words, his churros have been getting better and better every day for almost 50 years now – just to give you an idea of how perfectly crispy and tender each mouthful is. We recommend coming here early in the morning, as soon as the oil starts heating up – so you'll have the privilege of savouring the first batches of the day.

 CHURRERÍA SAN ROMÁN
CARRER DEL CONSELL DE CENT, 211
08002 BARCELONA

MON-SUN: 8am / 3pm – 5pm / 9pm

3. ASPIRIN IN AN ART NOUVEAU SETTING

Yes, a pharmacy can be worth going out of your way for.

Farmacia Aguilar Pérez already stands out because of its modernist façade alone. Inside, in an interior covered with Art nouveau-style carved wood panels, you'll find everything you could need to help you recover from a paella overdose or long night out.

While we don't recommend it, we understand how incredibly tempting it is to take a few pictures. Then again, they could have a placebo effect – that's how therapeutic the decor here is.

 FARMÀCIA AGUILAR PÉREZ
CARRER D'AUSIÀS MARC, 31
08010 BARCELONA

MON–FRI: 8am / 9:30pm
SAT: 9:30am / 2:30pm
SUN: Closed

4. THE CITY'S CALENDAR OF EVENTS

Barcelona's neighbourhoods are a reflection of its *trencadís*: like mosaics, they each have their own personality, traditions, and above all festivals. With some luck, you'll have a chance to get to know the soul of these neighbourhoods and their inhabitants during your stay.

MARCH

> The weekend closest to 23 March: Barri del Pi.

APRIL

> Mid-April : Sagrada Familia.
> 23 April: Sant Jordi. World Book Day.

MAY

> 2nd half of the month: Eixample derecho.

JULY

> 1st half of the month: Vila Olímpica.
> 2nd half of the month: : Poblesec.
> Mid-July: El Raval.

AUGUST

> 2nd half of the month: Gràcia.
> 2nd half of the month: Sants.
> Mid-August: Barrio Gótico.

SEPTEMBER

> 1st half of the month: La Ribera
> 1st half of the month: Poblenou Primera.
> 1st half of the month: Horta.
> The week of 24 September: Fiestas de la Mercè. A major festival that happens across the entire city.

OCTOBER

> 1st half of the month: Sarrià.
> 1st half of the month: La Rambla.
> 1st half of the month: Eixample Izquierdo.

NOVEMBER

> 1st half of the month: El Clot.

THE ROOFTOPS
OF BARCELONA

In Barcelona, it is of course impossible to go higher
than the tallest tower of Sagrada Familia, which rises to 172 metres.
Despite this limitation, Barcelona has many skyscrapers
scattered throughout the city.

These include some with sublime rooftops from
where you can admire Barcelona from on high.

1/ Located on a busy street, the Grand Central Hotel has a rooftop you can't detect from the outside. Dare to enter the hotel and proceed to the elevators to go up to the Skybar, where you can enjoy a glass of wine while you take in the view of the infinity pool and city.

2/ For a sky-high and festive evening, head to the rooftop of Hotel Pulitzer in summer (through late September). Five days a week, the hotel organises parties starting at 6 pm, with good music, tapas, and cocktails.

3/ The latest addition is the rooftop of the Barcelona Edition, where greenery and wooden elements make for a warm atmosphere.

1/ THE SKYBAR, AT THE GRAND CENTRAL HOTEL

2/ HOTEL PULITZER

3/ BARCELONA EDITION HOTEL'S ROOFTOP

EAT AT A
FISHMONGER'S SHOP

This fishmonger's shop invites you to sit down to eat.

In other words, you can choose the fish that strikes your fancy from the display, the sauce you'd like to eat it with, and it will be prepared and served to you precisely according to your wishes.

It doesn't get much fresher than that!

 LA PARADETA SAGRADA FAMÍLIA
PASSATGE SIMÓ, 18
08025 BARCELONA

TUE–THU: 1pm / 4pm – 8pm / 11:30pm FRI–SAT: 1pm / 4pm – 8pm / midnight SUN: 1pm / 4pm – 8pm / 11:30pm MON: Closed	+34 934 500 191	laparadeta.com

VINTAGE
CHIC

People come here all the way from Hollywood in the hopes of unearthing unique items from the 1920s, like flapper dresses. Even the iconic ball gown Rose wears in *Titanic* (1997) was dug up here – to give you an idea of just how rich a source of treasures and authenticity L'Arca is.

Carmen Viña was one of the first to open a second-hand boutique in Barcelona, making a name for herself and establishing a solid reputation, to the point that she's even dressed celebrities around the world. Today, her daughters Carmina Pairet and Nina Balmes even offer to design and tailor bespoke evening and wedding gowns using vintage fabrics and lace and other charming trimmings.

 L'ARCA
CARRER DELS BANYS NOUS, 20
08002 BARCELONA

MON-SAT: 11am / 2pm – 4:30pm / 8:30pm
SUN: Closed

BEHIND THE FRIDGE,
DECADENT COCKTAILS

On one side: a *pastrami* stand.

On the other: a secret cocktail bar. Just open the refrigerator door and take the secret passage to discover surprising flavours served in far-fetched glasses. You can definitely trust the mixologists when they recommend their craziest cocktail of the moment.

PARADISO
CARRER DE RERA PALAU, 4
08003 BARCELONA

MON-SUN: 7pm / 2:30am

paradiso.cat

- EL EQUIPO CREATIVO -

Oliver Franz Schmidt, Natali Canas del Pozo, and Lucas Echeveste Lacy are three architects who together form the studio El Equipo Creativo. In particular, they create spaces for our favourite activity: eating. We met them through Ferran and his brother Albert Adrià when they were designing the restaurant Tickets.

If you had to describe Barcelona in three words, what would they be?

Spontaneous, brilliant, laid back.

In what way does a project like Tickets reflect the soul of Barcelona?

You can feel it in the eclectic choice of furniture and finishes, together with the strategy of creating small bars that are reminiscent of market stalls. Preparing the food and eating there creates a real relationship between the guests and cook because they are so close to each other physically. That makes for a laid-back and festive atmosphere – a quality inherent to the soul of Barcelona.

What place or experience in Barcelona would El Equipo Creativo consider a must?

I'd recommend going to the El Poblenou neighbourhood, which also happens to be where our architecture studio is located. It's a former industrial district that's going through a major transformation, with former warehouses and factories now existing side-by-side with little boutiques and up-and-coming restaurants.

This mix makes it the perfect place to immerse yourself in the local atmosphere, far from the city's most touristy spots.

What's your favourite place to find inspiration for your projects?

La Central's bookshops, which are located in various neighbourhoods in the city. They're like black holes: If you enter prepare to be sucked in, because the books and magazines you'll find here are each more inspiring than the next, making it incredibly difficult to leave again.

**We never reveal the 31st address
in the Soul of series because it's strictly confidential.
Up to you to find it!**

MICRO-THEATRE:
15 MINUTES, 15 PEOPLE, 15 METRES

All the world's a stage, Shakespeare famously said. Who knows what he would have thought about Barcelona's stages, which are ready to surprise you anywhere? Microteatre Barcelona – a collective of eight small theatres with actors who get dangerously close to their small group of spectators – has all the elements of a contemporary art performance. You'll only find out where you need to go to see the performance *after* you've bought your tickets online. Art has never been more alive than this!

microteatrebarcelona.cat

MANY THANKS TO

JÉRÔME for introducing me to Barcelona and for accompanying me on all my explorations.

NOÉ for unflaggingly tasting all the pasta in town.

VINCENT AND JUAN for enrapturing the soul of this city in drawing and image.

EMMANUELLE AND NATHALIE for doing and undoing this book with patience and passion.

XAVI ALBA for finding us tables that did not exist in Albert's restaurants.

THOMAS JONGLEZ our expedition leader.

This book was created by:

Vincent Moustache, co-author and illustrator

Fany Péchiodat, co-author

Juan Jerez, photographer

Nathalie Chebou-Moth, publishing manager

Emmanuelle Willard Toulemonde, layout

Sophie Schlondorff, translator

Kimberly Bess, proofreading

You can write to us at contact@soul-of-cities.com

Follow us on Instagram on @soul_of_guides

In accordance with regularly upheld French jurisprudence (Toulouse 14-01-1887), the publisher will not be deemed responsible for any involuntary errors or omissions that may subsist in this guide despite our diligence and verifications by the editorial staff.

Any reproduction of the content, or part of the content, of this book by whatever means is forbidden without prior authorization by the publisher.

© JONGLEZ 2020
Registration of copyright: July 2020 - Edition: 01
ISBN: 978-2-36195-387-4
Printed in Slovakia by Polygraf